I Like to Read® books, created by award-winning picture book artists as well as talented newcomers, instill confidence and the joy of reading in new readers.

We want to hear every new reader say, "I like to read!"

Visit our website for flash cards, activities, and more about the series:
www.holidayhouse.com/ILiketoRead
#ILTR

This book has been officially leveled by using the
F&P Text Level Gradient™ Leveling System.

IT IS TIME

The Life of a Caterpillar

Lizzy Rockwell

I Like to Read®

HOLIDAY HOUSE • NEW YORK

For Miles and Wesley

The butterfly in this book is a black swallowtail butterfly.
The publisher thanks Hazel Davies, Director of Living Exhibits,
American Museum of Natural History, for her expert review of this book.

I LIKE TO READ is a registered trademark of Holiday House Publishing, Inc.

HOLIDAY HOUSE is registered in the U.S. Patent and Trademark Office.
Printed and bound in January 2023 at RR Donnelley, Dongguan, China.
The artwork was created with watercolor washes and digital tools.
www.holidayhouse.com
First Edition
1 3 5 7 9 10 8 6 4 2

This book has been officially leveled by using the F&P Text Level Gradient™ Leveling System.

Library of Congress Cataloging-in-Publication Data

Names: Rockwell, Lizzy, author.
Title: It is time : the life of a caterpillar / Lizzy Rockwell.
Description: First edition. | New York : Holiday House, [2023] | "I Like to
Read"—title page verso. | Audience: Ages 4–8 | Audience: Grades K–1 |
Summary: "A caterpillar hatches out of an egg and grows into
a butterfly through its life cycle"—Provided by publisher.
Identifiers: LCCN 2022015001 | ISBN 9780823450794 (hardcover)
Subjects: LCSH: Caterpillars—Juvenile literature. | Butterflies—Life cycles—Juvenile literature.
Classification: LCC QL544.2 .R638 2023 | DDC 595.7813/92—dc23/eng/20220429
LC record available at https://lccn.loc.gov/2022015001

ISBN: 978-0-8234-5079-4 (hardcover)

Egg

This is the egg.
Caterpillar is in it.

Caterpillar comes out.

She eats the egg.

She eats the leaf.
She poops.
She grows.

Her skin does
not grow.
It sheds.
And sheds.
And sheds.
And sheds.

Day 1

Day 3

Day 7

Day 10

Day 12

The bird wants to eat her.

What can
Caterpillar do?

She scares the bird!

It is time to change.
Caterpillar makes silk.
She hangs from
a stem.

She twists.
She turns.

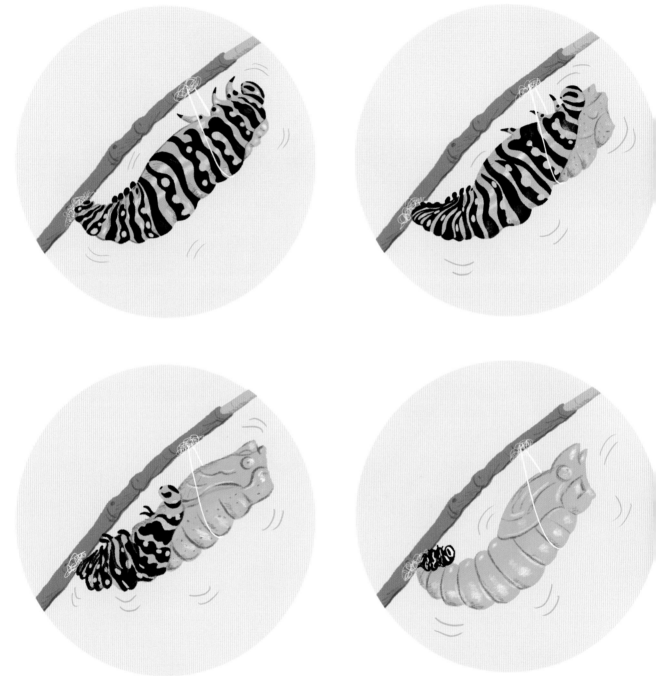

She sheds one last time.

A pupa is there.

Wind comes.

Rain comes.

The pupa is still there.

One day the pupa shakes.
It cracks.

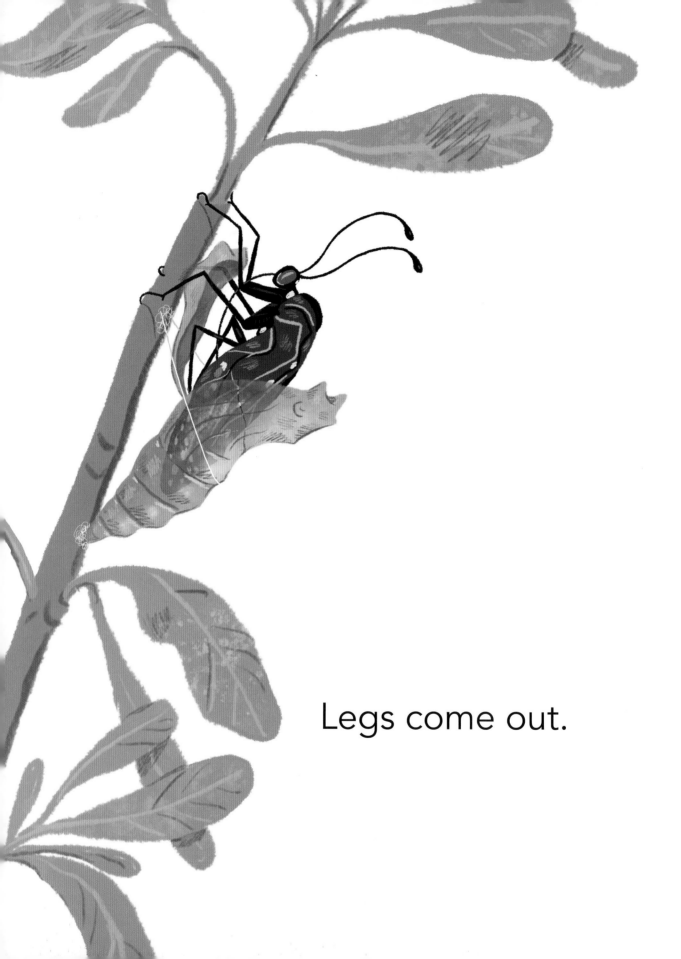

Legs come out.

Wings unfold.
They dry.

Fly, Butterfly!

Egg

Day 3

Day 30
(Later)

Day 30

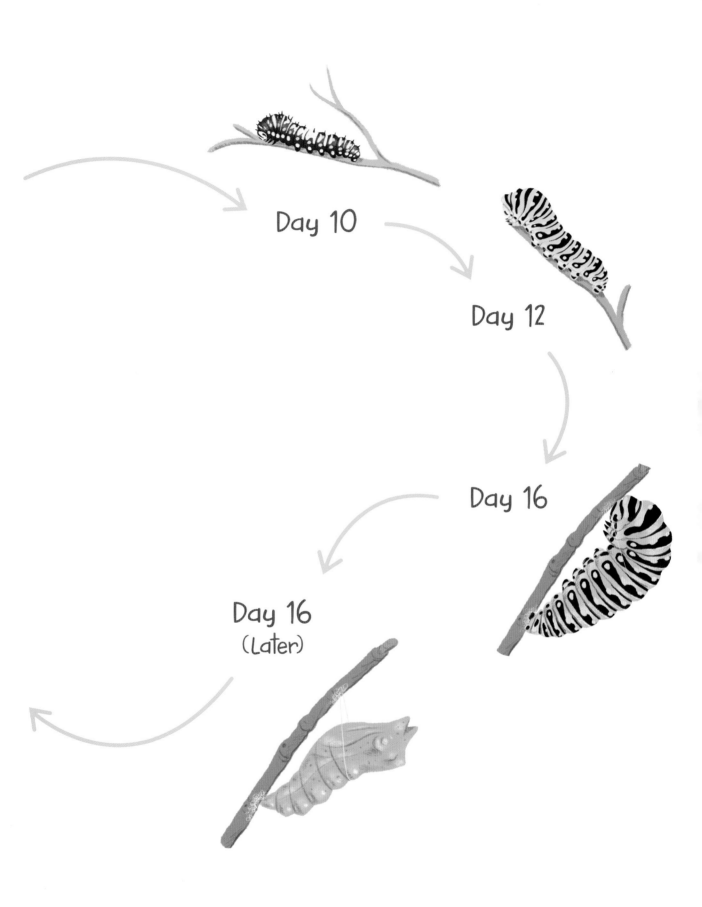

Day 10

Day 12

Day 16

Day 16
(Later)